for

_____

from

_____

*The fruit of the Spirit is love,
joy, peace, patience, kindness,
goodness, faithfulness,
gentleness and self-control.
Against such things there
is no law.*

—Galatians 5:22–23 (NIV)

Authentic Publishing
We welcome your questions and comments.

USA	1820 Jet Stream Drive, Colorado Springs, CO 80921
	www.authenticbooks.com
UK	9 Holdom Avenue, Bletchley, Milton Keynes, Bucks, MK1
	1QR
	www.authenticmedia.co.uk
India	Logos Bhavan, Medchal Road, Jeedimetla Village,
	Secunderabad
	500 055, A.P.

God's Promises on the Fruit of the Spirit
ISBN 978-1-934068-99-1

Copyright © 2008 by The Livingstone Corporation

Livingstone project staff includes Andy Culbertson, Linda Taylor,
Joan Guest, Everett O'Bryan. Interior design by Lindsay Galvin and
Larry Taylor.

Published in 2008 by Authentic.
All rights reserved.

A catalog record for this book is available from the Library of Congress.

Printed in the United States of America

GOD'S PROMISES

on the Fruit of the Spirit

CONTENTS

*The Blessings of Bearing
the Fruit of the Holy Spirit*

The Fruit

OF THE HOLY SPIRIT

I have told you these things so that you can have the true happiness that I have. I want you to be completely happy.

—John 15:11 (ERV)

Love

Jesus answered, "'You must love the Lord your God. You must love him with all your heart, all your soul, and all your mind.' This is the first and most important command. And the second command is like the first: 'You must love other people the same as you love yourself.'"

—*Matthew 22:37–39 (ERV)*

And so we know and rely on the love God has for us. God is love. Whoever lives in love lives in God, and God in him.

—*1 John 4:16 (NIV)*

Most important of all, continue to show deep love for each other, for love covers a multitude of sins.

—*1 Peter 4:8 (NLT)*

For the commandments say, "You must not commit adultery. You must not murder. You must not steal. You must not covet." These—and other such commandments—are summed up in this one commandment: "Love your neighbor as yourself." Love does no wrong to others, so love fulfills the requirements of God's law.

   —Romans 13:9–10 (NLT)

This is my prayer for you: that your love will grow more and more; that you will have knowledge and understanding with your love.

   —Philippians 1:9 (ERV)

Dear friends, let us love one another, for love comes from God. Everyone who loves has been born of God and knows God. Whoever does not love does not know God, because God is love.

   —1 John 4:7–8 (NIV)

Sow for yourselves righteousness; reap in mercy; break up your fallow ground, for it is time to seek the LORD, till He comes and rains righteousness on you.
—*Hosea 10:12 (NKJV)*

This is how we know what love is: Jesus Christ laid down his life for us. And we ought to lay down our lives for our brothers. If anyone has material possessions and sees his brother in need but has no pity on him, how can the love of God be in him? Dear children, let us not love with words or tongue but with actions and in truth.
—*1 John 3:16–18 (NIV)*

Let us think of ways to motivate one another to acts of love and good works.
—*Hebrews 10:24 (NLT)*

Keep on loving each other as brothers.
—*Hebrews 13:1 (NIV)*

If a person knows my commands and obeys those commands, then that person truly loves me. And my Father will love the person that loves me. And I will love that person. I will show myself to him.

—*John 14:21 (ERV)*

This is My commandment, that you love one another as I have loved you. Greater love has no one than this, than to lay down one's life for his friends.

—*John 15:12–13 (NKJV)*

I say to you people that are listening to me, love your enemies. Do good to those people that hate you. Ask God to bless those people that say bad things to you. Pray for those people that are mean to you.

—*Luke 6:27–28 (ERV)*

I pray that you, being rooted and established in love, may have power, together with all the saints, to grasp how wide and long and high and deep is the love of Christ.

—*Ephesians 3:17–18 (NIV)*

He loves righteousness and justice; the earth is full of the goodness of the LORD.

—*Psalm 33:5 (NKJV)*

God showed how much he loved us by sending his one and only Son into the world so that we might have eternal life through him. This is real love—not that we loved God, but that he loved us and sent his Son as a sacrifice to take away our sins.

—*1 John 4:9–10 (NLT)*

May your unfailing love rest upon us, O LORD, even as we put our hope in you.

—*Psalm 33:22 (NIV)*

I will praise You, O Lord, among the
peoples; I will sing to You among the
nations. For Your mercy reaches unto
the heavens, and Your truth unto the
clouds.
            —*Psalm 57:9–10 (NKJV)*

As the Father has loved me, so have
I loved you. Now remain in my love.
If you obey my commands, you will
remain in my love, just as I have obeyed
my Father's commands and remain in
his love.
            —*John 15:9–10 (NIV)*

A bowl of vegetables with someone you
love is better than steak with someone
you hate.
            —*Proverbs 15:17 (NLT)*

The person that always tries to show
love and kindness will have a good life,
wealth, and honor.
            —*Proverbs 21:21 (ERV)*

And may the Lord make you increase and abound in love to one another and to all, just as we do to you.

—*1 Thessalonians 3:12 (NKJV)*

Live a life filled with love, following the example of Christ. He loved us and offered himself as a sacrifice for us, a pleasing aroma to God.

—*Ephesians 5:2 (NLT)*

This is the message you heard from the beginning: We should love one another.

—*1 John 3:11 (NIV)*

Nevertheless let each one of you in particular so love his own wife as himself, and let the wife see that she respects her husband.

—*Ephesians 5:33 (NKJV)*

This is my command: Love each other.

—*John 15:17 (ERV)*

Do not seek revenge or bear a grudge against a fellow Israelite, but love your neighbor as yourself. I am the LORD.
—*Leviticus 19:18 (NLT)*

My brothers and sisters, God called you to be free. But don't use your freedom as an excuse to do the things that please your sinful selves. But serve each other with love. The whole law is made complete in this one command: "Love other people the same as you love yourself."
—*Galatians 5:13–14 (ERV)*

If you really fulfill the royal law according to the Scripture, "You shall love your neighbor as yourself," you do well.
—*James 2:8 (NKJV)*

A friend is always loyal, and a brother is born to help in time of need.
—*Proverbs 17:17 (NLT)*

So now I am giving you a new commandment: Love each other. Just as I have loved you, you should love each other. Your love for one another will prove to the world that you are my disciples.

—*John 13:34–35 (NLT)*

Hatred stirs up dissension, but love covers over all wrongs.

—*Proverbs 10:12 (NIV)*

Now you have made yourselves pure by obeying the truth. Now you can have true love for your brothers and sisters. So love each other deeply—with all your heart.

—*1 Peter 1:22 (ERV)*

No one has seen God at any time. If we love one another, God abides in us, and His love has been perfected in us.

—*1 John 4:12 (NKJV)*

Though I speak with the tongues of men and of angels, but have not love, I have become sounding brass or a clanging cymbal. And though I have the gift of prophecy, and understand all mysteries and all knowledge, and though I have all faith, so that I could remove mountains, but have not love, I am nothing. And though I bestow all my goods to feed the poor, and though I give my body to be burned, but have not love, it profits me nothing. Love suffers long and is kind; love does not envy; love does not parade itself, is not puffed up; does not behave rudely, does not seek its own, is not provoked, thinks no evil; does not rejoice in iniquity, but rejoices in the truth; bears all things, believes all things, hopes all things, endures all things. Love never fails. But whether there are prophecies, they will fail; whether there are

tongues, they will cease; whether there is knowledge, it will vanish away.
—1 Corinthians 13:1–8 (NKJV)

When a person is in Christ Jesus, it is not important if he is circumcised or not. The important thing is faith—the kind of faith that works through love.
—Galatians 5:6 (ERV)

For God so loved the world that he gave his one and only Son, that whoever believes in him shall not perish but have eternal life.
—John 3:16 (NIV)

And he has given us this command: Those who love God must also love their Christian brothers and sisters.
—1 John 4:21 (NLT)

Bear with each other and forgive whatever grievances you may have against one another. Forgive as the Lord forgave you. And over all these virtues put on love, which binds them all together in perfect unity.

—*Colossians 3:13–14 (NIV)*

PORTRAIT OF LOVE
JACOB *Loves* RACHEL

After Jacob had stayed with Laban
[his uncle] for about a month, Laban
said to him, "You shouldn't work for
me without pay just because we are
relatives. Tell me how much your wages
should be."

Now Laban had two daughters. The
older daughter was named Leah, and
the younger one was Rachel. There was
no sparkle in Leah's eyes, but Rachel
had a beautiful figure and a lovely face.
Since Jacob was in love with Rachel,
he told her father, "I'll work for you for
seven years if you'll give me Rachel,
your younger daughter, as my wife."

"Agreed!" Laban replied. "I'd rather
give her to you than to anyone else.
Stay and work with me." So Jacob

worked seven years to pay for Rachel.
But his love for her was so strong that
it seemed to him but a few days.

—*Genesis 29:14–20 (NLT)*

Joy

You will show me the way of life,
granting me the joy of your presence
and the pleasures of living with you
forever.

> —*Psalm 16:11 (NLT)*

The hope of the righteous will be
gladness, but the expectation of the
wicked will perish.

> —*Proverbs 10:28 (NKJV)*

But I trust in your unfailing love; my
heart rejoices in your salvation.

> —*Psalm 13:5 (NIV)*

Lord, you have made me very happy! I
am happier now than at harvest time—
when we celebrate because we have
much grain and wine.

> —*Psalm 4:7 (ERV)*

Therefore by Him let us continually offer the sacrifice of praise to God, that is, the fruit of our lips, giving thanks to His name.

—Hebrews 13:15 (NKJV)

But let all those rejoice who put their trust in You; let them ever shout for joy, because You defend them; let those also who love Your name be joyful in You. For You, O LORD, will bless the righteous; with favor You will surround him as with a shield.

—Psalm 5:11–12 (NKJV)

In the same way, there is joy in the presence of God's angels when even one sinner repents.

—Luke 15:10 (NLT)

A person that smiles makes other people happy. And good news makes people feel better.

—Proverbs 15:30 (ERV)

A happy heart makes the face cheerful,
but heartache crushes the spirit.
—*Proverbs 15:13 (NIV)*

But let the righteous be glad; let them
rejoice before God; yes, let them rejoice
exceedingly.
—*Psalm 68:3 (NKJV)*

Your unfailing love is better than life
itself; how I praise you! I will praise you
as long as I live, lifting up my hands to
you in prayer. You satisfy me more than
the richest feast. I will praise you with
songs of joy.
—*Psalm 63:3–5 (NLT)*

A good person is happy to serve the
Lord. He depends on God. And when
good honest people see what happens,
they praise the Lord!
—*Psalm 64:10 (ERV)*

Everything on earth, shout with joy to God! Praise his glorious name! Honor him with songs of praise! Tell God how wonderful his works are! God, your power is very great! Your enemies bow down. They are afraid of you!
—*Psalm 66:1–3 (ERV)*

Always be joyful.
—*1 Thessalonians 5:16 (NLT)*

When justice is done, it brings joy to the righteous but terror to evildoers.
—*Proverbs 21:15 (NIV)*

The Lord's laws are right. They make people happy. The Lord's commands are good. They show people the right way to live.
—*Psalm 19:8 (ERV)*

Deceit is in the heart of those who devise evil, but counselors of peace have joy.
—*Proverbs 12:20 (NKJV)*

The LORD is my strength and shield. I trust him with all my heart. He helps me, and my heart is filled with joy. I burst out in songs of thanksgiving.

—*Psalm 28:7 (NLT)*

Look to God for help. You will be accepted. Don't be ashamed.

—*Psalm 34:5 (ERV)*

Come, everyone! Clap your hands! Shout to God with joyful praise! For the LORD Most High is awesome. He is the great King of all the earth.

—*Psalm 47:1–2 (NLT)*

Rejoice in the Lord always. I will say it again: Rejoice!

—*Philippians 4:4 (NIV)*

He will once again fill your mouth with laughter and your lips with shouts of joy.

—*Job 8:21 (NLT)*

For His anger is but for a moment, His favor is for life; weeping may endure for a night, but joy comes in the morning.
—*Psalm 30:5 (NKJV)*

Light and happiness shine on good people.
—*Psalm 97:11 (ERV)*

But may all who seek you rejoice and be glad in you; may those who love your salvation always say, "Let God be exalted!"
—*Psalm 70:4 (NIV)*

The Lord will save his people. They will return to Zion with joy. They will be very, very happy. Their happiness will be like a crown on their heads forever. They will be singing with joy. All sadness will be gone far away.
—*Isaiah 51:11 (ERV)*

Your testimonies I have taken as
a heritage forever, for they are the
rejoicing of my heart.
        —*Psalm 119:111 (NKJV)*

A person might be sad when he plants
the seeds, but he will be happy when he
gathers the crops! He might cry when
he carries the seeds out to the field, but
he will be happy when he brings the
harvest in!
        —*Psalm 126:5–6 (ERV)*

You will live in joy and peace. The
mountains and hills will burst into
song, and the trees of the field will clap
their hands!
        —*Isaiah 55:12 (NLT)*

I have rejoiced in your laws as much as
in riches.
        —*Psalm 119:14 (NLT)*

Blessed are you when men hate you,
when they exclude you and insult you
and reject your name as evil, because
of the Son of Man. Rejoice in that day
and leap for joy, because great is your
reward in heaven. For that is how their
fathers treated the prophets.
    —*Luke 6:22–23 (NIV)*

So be happy, people of Zion. Be joyful
in the Lord your God. He will be good
and give you rain. He will send you
the early rains and the late rains like
before.
    —*Joel 2:23 (ERV)*

For the kingdom of God is not a
matter of eating and drinking, but of
righteousness, peace and joy in the
Holy Spirit.
    —*Romans 14:17 (NIV)*

Even though the fig trees have no
blossoms, and there are no grapes
on the vines; even though the olive
crop fails, and the fields lie empty and
barren; even though the flocks die in
the fields, and the cattle barns are
empty, yet I will rejoice in the LORD! I
will be joyful in the God of my salvation!
 —*Habakkuk 3:17–18 (NLT)*

Until now you have asked nothing in
My name. Ask, and you will receive,
that your joy may be full.
 —*John 16:24 (NKJV)*

You taught me how to live. You will
come close to me and give me great joy.
 —*Acts 2:28 (ERV)*

And Nehemiah continued, "Go and celebrate with a feast of rich foods and sweet drinks, and share gifts of food with people who have nothing prepared. This is a sacred day before our Lord. Don't be dejected and sad, for the joy of the LORD is your strength!"

—*Nehemiah 8:10 (NLT)*

May the God of hope fill you with all joy and peace as you trust in him, so that you may overflow with hope by the power of the Holy Spirit.

—*Romans 15:13 (NIV)*

My enemies have surrounded me. But the Lord will help me defeat them! Then I will offer sacrifices in his tent. I will give the sacrifices with shouts of joy. I will sing and play songs to honor the Lord.

—*Psalm 27:6 (ERV)*

PORTRAIT OF JOY
A JAILER FINDS *Faith*

Then the multitude rose up together against [Paul and Silas]; and the magistrates tore off their clothes and commanded them to be beaten with rods. And when they had laid many stripes on them, they threw them into prison, commanding the jailer to keep them securely. Having received such a charge, he put them into the inner prison and fastened their feet in the stocks.

But at midnight Paul and Silas were praying and singing hymns to God, and the prisoners were listening to them. Suddenly there was a great earthquake, so that the foundations of the prison were shaken; and immediately all the doors were opened and everyone's

chains were loosed. And the keeper
of the prison, awaking from sleep
and seeing the prison doors open,
supposing the prisoners had fled, drew
his sword and was about to kill himself.
But Paul called with a loud voice,
saying, "Do yourself no harm, for we
are all here."

Then he called for a light, ran in,
and fell down trembling before Paul
and Silas. And he brought them out
and said, "Sirs, what must I do to be
saved?"

So they said, "Believe on the Lord
Jesus Christ, and you will be saved,
you and your household." Then they
spoke the word of the Lord to him
and to all who were in his house. And
he took them the same hour of the
night and washed their stripes. And
immediately he and all his family were
baptized. Now when he had brought

them into his house, he set food before them; and he rejoiced, having believed in God with all his household.

—*Acts 16:22–34 (NKJV)*

Peace

Be anxious for nothing, but in everything by prayer and supplication, with thanksgiving, let your requests be made known to God; and the peace of God, which surpasses all understanding, will guard your hearts and minds through Christ Jesus.

—Philippians 4:6–7 (NKJV)

And let the peace of God rule in your hearts, to which also you were called in one body; and be thankful.

—Colossians 3:15 (NKJV)

Find rest, O my soul, in God alone; my hope comes from him. He alone is my rock and my salvation; he is my fortress, I will not be shaken.

—Psalm 62:5–6 (NIV)

A heart at peace gives life to the body, but envy rots the bones.
—*Proverbs 14:30 (NIV)*

Then Jesus said, "Come to me, all of you who are weary and carry heavy burdens, and I will give you rest."
—*Matthew 11:28 (NLT)*

Christ came and preached peace to you people (non-Jews) who were far away from God. And he preached peace to the people (Jews) who were near to God.
—*Ephesians 2:17 (ERV)*

Make every effort to keep the unity of the Spirit through the bond of peace.
—*Ephesians 4:3 (NIV)*

Be at peace among yourselves.
—*1 Thessalonians 5:13 (NKJV)*

May the Lord protect his people. May the Lord bless his people with peace.
—*Psalm 29:11 (ERV)*

I prayed to the LORD, and he answered me. He freed me from all my fears.
—*Psalm 34:4 (NLT)*

So Jesus said to them again, "Peace to you! As the Father has sent Me, I also send you."
—*John 20:21 (NKJV)*

I keep the Lord before me always. And I will never leave his right side. So my heart and soul will be very happy. Even my body will live in safety.
—*Psalm 16:8–9 (ERV)*

Peace I leave with you; my peace I give you. I do not give to you as the world gives. Do not let your hearts be troubled and do not be afraid.
—*John 14:27 (NIV)*

God's power is complete. The Lord's word has been tested. He protects people who trust him.
—*Psalm 18:30 (ERV)*

He makes me to lie down in green pastures; He leads me beside the still waters. He restores my soul; He leads me in the paths of righteousness for His name's sake. Yea, though I walk through the valley of the shadow of death, I will fear no evil; for You are with me; Your rod and Your staff, they comfort me.

—*Psalm 23:2–4 (NKJV)*

Truly my soul silently waits for God; from Him comes my salvation.

—*Psalm 62:1 (NKJV)*

Then He said to His disciples, "Therefore I say to you, do not worry about your life, what you will eat; nor about the body, what you will put on. Life is more than food, and the body is more than clothing."

—*Luke 12:22–23 (NKJV)*

But the wisdom from above is first of all pure. It is also peace loving, gentle at all times, and willing to yield to others. It is full of mercy and good deeds. It shows no favoritism and is always sincere. And those who are peacemakers will plant seeds of peace and reap a harvest of righteousness.
        —*James 3:17–18 (NLT)*

Lord, you will grant us peace; all we have accomplished is really from you.
        —*Isaiah 26:12 (NLT)*

Give all your worries to him, because he cares for you.
        —*1 Peter 5:7 (ERV)*

Whatever you have learned or received or heard from me, or seen in me—put it into practice. And the God of peace will be with you.
        —*Philippians 4:9 (NIV)*

But now you have been united with Christ Jesus. Once you were far away from God, but now you have been brought near to him through the blood of Christ. For Christ himself has brought peace to us. He united Jews and Gentiles into one people when, in his own body on the cross, he broke down the wall of hostility that separated us. He did this by ending the system of law with its commandments and regulations. He made peace between Jews and Gentiles by creating in himself one new people from the two groups.

—Ephesians 2:13–15 (NLT)

In peace I will lie down and sleep, for you alone, O LORD, will keep me safe.

—Psalm 4:8 (NLT)

God will give trouble and suffering to every person that does evil—to the Jews first and also to the non-Jews. But God will give glory, honor, and peace to every person that does good—to the Jews first and also to the non-Jews.
—Romans 2:9–10 (ERV)

Depart from evil and do good; seek peace and pursue it.
—Psalm 34:14 (NKJV)

You will keep in perfect peace him whose mind is steadfast, because he trusts in you.
—Isaiah 26:3 (NIV)

Humble people will get the land God promised. And they will enjoy peace.
—Psalm 37:11 (ERV)

Those who love your instructions have great peace and do not stumble.
—Psalm 119:165 (NLT)

For, "Whoever would love life and see good days must keep his tongue from evil and his lips from deceitful speech. He must turn from evil and do good; he must seek peace and pursue it."
—*1 Peter 3:10–11 (NIV)*

Finally, brothers, good-by. Aim for perfection, listen to my appeal, be of one mind, live in peace. And the God of love and peace will be with you.
—*2 Corinthians 13:11 (NIV)*

If it is possible, as much as depends on you, live peaceably with all men.
—*Romans 12:18 (NKJV)*

So then, let us aim for harmony in the church and try to build each other up.
—*Romans 14:19 (NLT)*

Now, Job, give yourself to God and make peace with him. Do this, and you will get many good things.
—*Job 22:21 (ERV)*

PORTRAIT OF PEACE
ELISHA *Trusts* GOD

The king of Aram was making war against Israel. He had a council meeting with his army officers. He said, "Hide in this place and attack the Israelites when they come by."

But the man of God (Elisha) sent a message to the king of Israel. Elisha said, "Be careful! Don't go by that place! The Aramean soldiers are hiding there!" The king of Israel sent a message to his men at the place that the man of God (Elisha) warned him about. And the king of Israel saved quite a few men.

The king of Aram was very upset about this. The king of Aram called his army officers and said to them, "Tell me who is spying for the king of Israel." One of the officers of the king of Aram said, "My lord and king, not one of us is a spy! Elisha, the prophet from Israel, can tell the king of Israel many secret things—even the words that you speak in your bedroom!" The king of Aram said, "Find Elisha and I will send men to catch him!" The servants told the king of Aram, "Elisha is in Dothan!"

Then the king of Aram sent horses, chariots, and a large army to Dothan. They arrived at night and surrounded the city. Elisha's servant got up early that morning. The servant went outside, and he saw an army with horses and chariots all around the city! Elisha's servant said to Elisha, "Oh, my master, what can we do?"

Elisha said, "Don't be afraid! The army that fights for us is larger than the army that fights for Aram!" Then Elisha prayed and said, "Lord, I ask you, open my servant's eyes so he can see." The Lord opened the eyes of the young man, and the servant saw the mountain was full of horses and chariots of fire. They were all around Elisha!

—*2 Kings 6:8–17 (ERV)*

Patience

Wait on the LORD; be of good courage,
and He shall strengthen your heart;
wait, I say, on the LORD!
—*Psalm 27:14 (NKJV)*

Be still before the LORD and wait
patiently for him; do not fret when men
succeed in their ways, when they carry
out their wicked schemes.
—*Psalm 37:7 (NIV)*

Consider it pure joy, my brothers,
whenever you face trials of many kinds,
because you know that the testing
of your faith develops perseverance.
Perseverance must finish its work so
that you may be mature and complete,
not lacking anything.
—*James 1:2–4 (NIV)*

God, create a pure heart in me! Make my spirit strong again!
—*Psalm 51:10 (ERV)*

As for the rest of you, dear brothers and sisters, never get tired of doing good.
—*2 Thessalonians 3:13 (NLT)*

Be of good courage, and He shall strengthen your heart, all you who hope in the LORD.
—*Psalm 31:24 (NKJV)*

Don't be angry! Don't get mad! Don't become so upset that you also want to do bad things.
—*Psalm 37:8 (ERV)*

May the Lord direct your hearts into God's love and Christ's perseverance.
—*2 Thessalonians 3:5 (NIV)*

So then, my beloved brethren, let every man be swift to hear, slow to speak, slow to wrath.

—*James 1:19 (NKJV)*

Finishing is better than starting. Patience is better than pride. Control your temper, for anger labels you a fool.

—*Ecclesiastes 7:8–9 (NLT)*

So it is good to wait quietly for salvation from the LORD.

—*Lamentations 3:26 (NLT)*

To those who by persistence in doing good seek glory, honor and immortality, he will give eternal life.

—*Romans 2:7 (NIV)*

And not only that, but we also glory in tribulations, knowing that tribulation produces perseverance; and perseverance, character; and character, hope.

—*Romans 5:3–4 (NKJV)*

But we are hoping for something that we don't have yet. We are waiting for it patiently.

—*Romans 8:25 (ERV)*

I wait for the Lord, my soul waits, and in his word I put my hope. My soul waits for the Lord more than watchmen wait for the morning, more than watchmen wait for the morning.

—*Psalm 130:5–6 (NIV)*

Yes, in the way of Your judgments, O LORD, we have waited for You; the desire of our soul is for Your name and for the remembrance of You.

—*Isaiah 26:8 (NKJV)*

You need to persevere so that when you have done the will of God, you will receive what he has promised.

—*Hebrews 10:36 (NIV)*

But you are a man of God. So you should stay away from all those things. Try to live in the right way, serve God, have faith, love, patience, and gentleness.
—*1 Timothy 6:11 (ERV)*

Therefore, since we are surrounded by such a huge crowd of witnesses to the life of faith, let us strip off every weight that slows us down, especially the sin that so easily trips us up. And let us run with endurance the race God has set before us.
—*Hebrews 12:1 (NLT)*

Let us not become weary in doing good, for at the proper time we will reap a harvest if we do not give up.
—*Galatians 6:9 (NIV)*

Brothers and sisters, be patient; the Lord Jesus will come. So be patient until that time. Farmers are patient. A farmer waits for his valuable crop to grow up from the earth. A farmer waits patiently for his crop to receive the first rain and the last rain. You must be patient, too. Don't stop hoping. The Lord Jesus is coming soon.
—*James 5:7–8 (ERV)*

[We pray] that you may walk worthy of the Lord, fully pleasing Him, being fruitful in every good work and increasing in the knowledge of God; strengthened with all might, according to His glorious power, for all patience and longsuffering with joy.
—*Colossians 1:10–11 (NKJV)*

[Be] patient in tribulation, continuing steadfastly in prayer.
—*Romans 12:12 (NKJV)*

Brothers and sisters, we urge you to warn those who are lazy. Encourage those who are timid. Take tender care of those who are weak. Be patient with everyone.

—1 Thessalonians 5:14 (NLT)

In view of all this, make every effort to respond to God's promises. Supplement your faith with a generous provision of moral excellence, and moral excellence with knowledge, and knowledge with self-control, and self-control with patient endurance, and patient endurance with godliness.

—2 Peter 1:5–6 (NLT)

Be completely humble and gentle; be patient, bearing with one another in love.

—Ephesians 4:2 (NIV)

But for that very reason I was shown mercy so that in me, the worst of sinners, Christ Jesus might display his unlimited patience as an example for those who would believe on him and receive eternal life.

—*1 Timothy 1:16 (NIV)*

You said, "The Lord is slow to become angry. The Lord is full of great love. The Lord forgives people who are guilty and break the law. But the Lord always punishes people who are guilty. The Lord punishes those people, and he also punishes their children, their grandchildren, and even their great-grandchildren for those bad things!"

—*Numbers 14:18 (ERV)*

Therefore the LORD will wait, that He may be gracious to you; and therefore He will be exalted, that He may have mercy on you. For the LORD is a God of justice; blessed are all those who wait for Him.

—*Isaiah 30:18 (NKJV)*

The Lord isn't really being slow about his promise, as some people think. No, he is being patient for your sake. He does not want anyone to be destroyed, but wants everyone to repent.

—*2 Peter 3:9 (NLT)*

PORTRAIT OF PATIENCE
JOB *Perseveres*

There was a man in the land of Uz, whose name was Job; and that man was blameless and upright, and one who feared God and shunned evil. And seven sons and three daughters were born to him. Also, his possessions were seven thousand sheep, three thousand camels, five hundred yoke of oxen, five hundred female donkeys, and a very large household, so that this man was the greatest of all the people of the East. . . .

Then the LORD said to Satan, "Have you considered My servant Job, that there is none like him on the earth, a blameless and upright man, one who fears God and shuns evil?"

So Satan answered the LORD and said, "Does Job fear God for nothing?

Have You not made a hedge around him, around his household, and around all that he has on every side? You have blessed the work of his hands, and his possessions have increased in the land. But now, stretch out Your hand and touch all that he has, and he will surely curse You to Your face!"

And the LORD said to Satan, "Behold, all that he has is in your power; only do not lay a hand on his person."

So Satan went out from the presence of the LORD.

Now there was a day when his sons and daughters were eating and drinking wine in their oldest brother's house; and a messenger came to Job and said, "The oxen were plowing and the donkeys feeding beside them, when the Sabeans raided them and took them away—indeed they have killed the servants with the edge of the sword;

and I alone have escaped to tell you!"

While he was still speaking, another also came and said, "The fire of God fell from heaven and burned up the sheep and the servants, and consumed them; and I alone have escaped to tell you!"

While he was still speaking, another also came and said, "The Chaldeans formed three bands, raided the camels and took them away, yes, and killed the servants with the edge of the sword; and I alone have escaped to tell you!"

While he was still speaking, another also came and said, "Your sons and daughters were eating and drinking wine in their oldest brother's house, and suddenly a great wind came from across the wilderness and struck the four corners of the house, and it fell on the young people, and they are dead; and I alone have escaped to tell you!"

Then Job arose, tore his robe, and

shaved his head; and he fell to the ground and worshiped. And he said: "Naked I came from my mother's womb, and naked shall I return there. The LORD gave, and the LORD has taken away; blessed be the name of the LORD." In all this Job did not sin nor charge God with wrong. . . .

Then the LORD said to Satan, "Have you considered My servant Job, that there is none like him on the earth, a blameless and upright man, one who fears God and shuns evil? And still he holds fast to his integrity, although you incited Me against him, to destroy him without cause."

So Satan answered the LORD and said, "Skin for skin! Yes, all that a man has he will give for his life. But stretch out Your hand now, and touch his bone and his flesh, and he will surely curse You to Your face!"

And the LORD said to Satan, "Behold, he is in your hand, but spare his life."

So Satan went out from the presence of the LORD, and struck Job with painful boils from the sole of his foot to the crown of his head. And he took for himself a potsherd with which to scrape himself while he sat in the midst of the ashes.

Then his wife said to him, "Do you still hold fast to your integrity? Curse God and die!" But he said to her, "You speak as one of the foolish women speaks. Shall we indeed accept good from God, and shall we not accept adversity?" In all this Job did not sin with his lips.

—from Job 1:1–2:10 (NKJV)

Kindness

Because you have these blessings,
you should try as much as you can
to add these things to your life: to
your faith add goodness; and to your
goodness add knowledge; and to your
knowledge add self-control; and to your
self-control add patience; and to your
patience add service for God; and to
your service for God add kindness for
your brothers and sisters in Christ; and
to this kindness for your brothers and
sisters add love.
—*2 Peter 1:5–7 (ERV)*

The person that causes trouble for poor
people shows that he does not respect
God—God made both people. But if a
person is kind to poor people, then he
shows honor to God.
—*Proverbs 14:31 (ERV)*

Share with God's people who are in
need. Practice hospitality.
—*Romans 12:13 (NIV)*

One day some parents brought their
children to Jesus so he could touch and
bless them. But the disciples scolded
the parents for bothering him. When
Jesus saw what was happening, he
was angry with his disciples. He said
to them, "Let the children come to me.
Don't stop them! For the Kingdom of
God belongs to those who are like these
children. I tell you the truth, anyone
who doesn't receive the Kingdom of God
like a child will never enter it." Then
he took the children in his arms and
placed his hands on their heads and
blessed them.
—*Mark 10:13–16 (NLT)*

Remember this—a farmer who plants only a few seeds will get a small crop. But the one who plants generously will get a generous crop.

—*2 Corinthians 9:6 (NLT)*

But encourage one another daily, as long as it is called Today, so that none of you may be hardened by sin's deceitfulness.

—*Hebrews 3:13 (NIV)*

Share your homes with each other without complaining.

—*1 Peter 4:9 (ERV)*

Pleasant words are like a honeycomb, sweetness to the soul and health to the bones.

—*Proverbs 16:24 (NKJV)*

Blessed are the merciful, for they will be shown mercy.

—*Matthew 5:7 (NIV)*

Then he turned to his host. "When you put on a luncheon or a banquet," he said, "don't invite your friends, brothers, relatives, and rich neighbors. For they will invite you back, and that will be your only reward. Instead, invite the poor, the crippled, the lame, and the blind. Then at the resurrection of the righteous, God will reward you for inviting those who could not repay you."

—*Luke 14:12–14 (NLT)*

Gentle words are a tree of life; a deceitful tongue crushes the spirit.

—*Proverbs 15:4 (NLT)*

Therefore, whatever you want men to do to you, do also to them, for this is the Law and the Prophets.

—*Matthew 7:12 (NKJV)*

Sell the things you have and give that money to people that need it. The riches of this world don't continue. So get the kind of riches that continue. Get the treasure of heaven. That treasure continues forever. Thieves can't steal your treasure in heaven, and moths can't destroy it.

—Luke 12:33 (ERV)

A gracious woman gains respect, but ruthless men gain only wealth.

—Proverbs 11:16 (NLT)

The LORD is gracious and righteous; our God is full of compassion.

—Psalm 116:5 (NIV)

He who has pity on the poor lends to the LORD, and He will pay back what he has given.

—Proverbs 19:17 (NKJV)

The LORD is like a father to his children, tender and compassionate to those who fear him.
—*Psalm 103:13 (NLT)*

Jesus saw the many people and felt sorry for them. Jesus felt sorry for the people because the people were worried and helpless. The people were like sheep without a shepherd to lead them.
—*Matthew 9:36 (ERV)*

Praise be to the God and Father of our Lord Jesus Christ, the Father of compassion and the God of all comfort.
—*2 Corinthians 1:3 (NIV)*

This is what the LORD of Heaven's Armies says: Judge fairly, and show mercy and kindness to one another.
—*Zechariah 7:9 (NLT)*

He who gives to the poor will not lack, but he who hides his eyes will have many curses.

—Proverbs 28:27 (NKJV)

If your enemy is hungry, give him food to eat. If your enemy is thirsty, give him water to drink.

—Proverbs 25:21 (ERV)

Rather, as servants of God we commend ourselves in every way: in great endurance; in troubles, hardships and distresses . . . in purity, understanding, patience and kindness; in the Holy Spirit and in sincere love.

—2 Corinthians 6:4, 6 (NIV)

And a servant of the Lord must not quarrel but be gentle to all, able to teach, patient.

—2 Timothy 2:24 (NKJV)

Then the King will say to those on His right hand, "Come, you blessed of My Father, inherit the kingdom prepared for you from the foundation of the world: for I was hungry and you gave Me food; I was thirsty and you gave Me drink; I was a stranger and you took Me in; I was naked and you clothed Me; I was sick and you visited Me; I was in prison and you came to Me."

Then the righteous will answer Him, saying, "Lord, when did we see You hungry and feed You, or thirsty and give You drink? When did we see You a stranger and take You in, or naked and clothe You? Or when did we see You sick, or in prison, and come to You?" And the King will answer and say to them, "Assuredly, I say to you, inasmuch as you did it to one of the least of these My brethren, you did it to Me."

—Matthew 25:34–40 (NKJV)

Jesus saw the huge crowd as he stepped from the boat, and he had compassion on them and healed their sick.

—Matthew 14:14 (NLT)

Good will come to him who is generous and lends freely, who conducts his affairs with justice.

—Psalm 112:5 (NIV)

If any person helps one of these little ones because they are my followers, then that person will truly get his reward. That person will get his reward even if he only gave my follower a cup of cold water.

—Matthew 10:42 (ERV)

Share each other's burdens, and in this way obey the law of Christ.

—Galatians 6:2 (NLT)

But love your enemies, do good, and lend, hoping for nothing in return; and your reward will be great, and you will be sons of the Most High. For He is kind to the unthankful and evil.
—*Luke 6:35 (NKJV)*

Be sure that no person pays back wrong for wrong. But always try to do what is good for each other and for all people.
—*1 Thessalonians 5:15 (ERV)*

PORTRAIT OF KINDNESS
THE *Good* SAMARITAN

In reply Jesus said: "A man was going
down from Jerusalem to Jericho, when
he fell into the hands of robbers. They
stripped him of his clothes, beat him
and went away, leaving him half dead.
A priest happened to be going down the
same road, and when he saw the man,
he passed by on the other side. So too,
a Levite, when he came to the place and
saw him, passed by on the other side.
But a Samaritan, as he traveled, came
where the man was; and when he saw
him, he took pity on him. He went to
him and bandaged his wounds, pouring
on oil and wine. Then he put the man
on his own donkey, took him to an
inn and took care of him. The next
day he took out two silver coins and
gave them to the innkeeper. 'Look after

him,' he said, 'and when I return, I will reimburse you for any extra expense you may have.'

"Which of these three do you think was a neighbor to the man who fell into the hands of robbers?"

The expert in the law replied, "The one who had mercy on him."

Jesus told him, "Go and do likewise."
—*Luke 10:30–37 (NIV)*

Goodness

In the same way, let your light shine before men, that they may see your good deeds and praise your Father in heaven.

—*Matthew 5:16 (NIV)*

If you are wise and understand God's ways, prove it by living an honorable life, doing good works with the humility that comes from wisdom.

—*James 3:13 (NLT)*

Pure and undefiled religion before God and the Father is this: to visit orphans and widows in their trouble, and to keep oneself unspotted from the world.

—*James 1:27 (NKJV)*

Take heed that you do not do your charitable deeds before men, to be seen by them. Otherwise you have no reward from your Father in heaven. Therefore, when you do a charitable deed, do not sound a trumpet before you as the hypocrites do in the synagogues and in the streets, that they may have glory from men. Assuredly, I say to you, they have their reward. But when you do a charitable deed, do not let your left hand know what your right hand is doing, that your charitable deed may be in secret; and your Father who sees in secret will Himself reward you openly.

—*Matthew 6:1–4 (NKJV)*

And don't forget to do good for other people. And share with other people. These are the sacrifices that please God.

—*Hebrews 13:16 (ERV)*

If you love those who love you, what credit is that to you? Even "sinners" love those who love them. And if you do good to those who are good to you, what credit is that to you? Even "sinners" do that. And if you lend to those from whom you expect repayment, what credit is that to you? Even "sinners" lend to "sinners," expecting to be repaid in full. But love your enemies, do good to them, and lend to them without expecting to get anything back. Then your reward will be great, and you will be sons of the Most High, because he is kind to the ungrateful and wicked.

—*Luke 6:32–35 (NIV)*

Never pay back evil with more evil. Do things in such a way that everyone can see you are honorable.

—*Romans 12:17 (NLT)*

Now may our Lord Jesus Christ Himself, and our God and Father, who has loved us and given us everlasting consolation and good hope by grace, comfort your hearts and establish you in every good word and work.

—*2 Thessalonians 2:16–17 (NKJV)*

If you refuse to do bad things, and if you do good things, then you will live forever. The Lord loves fairness. He will not leave his followers without help. The Lord will always protect his followers, but he will destroy wicked people.

—*Psalm 37:27–28 (ERV)*

Test everything that is said. Hold on to what is good. Stay away from every kind of evil.

—*1 Thessalonians 5:21–22 (NLT)*

Remind the people to be subject to rulers and authorities, to be obedient, to be ready to do whatever is good, to slander no one, to be peaceable and considerate, and to show true humility toward all men.

—*Titus 3:1–2 (NIV)*

Do not share in the sins of others. Keep yourself pure.

—*1 Timothy 5:22 (NIV)*

Whenever you can, do good things for people who need help.

—*Proverbs 3:27 (ERV)*

A good man out of the good treasure of his heart brings forth good; and an evil man out of the evil treasure of his heart brings forth evil. For out of the abundance of the heart his mouth speaks.

—*Luke 6:45 (NKJV)*

Don't let anyone look down on you because you are young, but set an example for the believers in speech, in life, in love, in faith and in purity.

—*1 Timothy 4:12 (NIV)*

If you plan to do evil, you will be lost; if you plan to do good, you will receive unfailing love and faithfulness.

—*Proverbs 14:22 (NLT)*

Then Peter opened his mouth and said: "In truth I perceive that God shows no partiality. But in every nation whoever fears Him and works righteousness is accepted by Him."

—*Acts 10:34–35 (NKJV)*

It is the same with faith. If faith does nothing, then that faith is dead, because it is alone.

—*James 2:17 (ERV)*

Surely goodness and love will follow me all the days of my life, and I will dwell in the house of the LORD forever.
    —*Psalm 23:6 (NIV)*

For the LORD God is a sun and shield; the LORD will give grace and glory; no good thing will He withhold from those who walk uprightly.
    —*Psalm 84:11 (NKJV)*

The goal of this command is love, which comes from a pure heart and a good conscience and a sincere faith.
    —*1 Timothy 1:5 (NIV)*

God has made us what we are. In Christ Jesus, God made us new people so that we would do good things. God had already planned those good things for us. God had planned for us to live our lives doing those good things.
    —*Ephesians 2:10 (ERV)*

Trust in the LORD, and do good;
dwell in the land, and feed on His
faithfulness.
—*Psalm 37:3 (NKJV)*

He has showed you, O man, what is
good. And what does the LORD require
of you? To act justly and to love mercy
and to walk humbly with your God.
—*Micah 6:8 (NIV)*

Choose a good reputation over great
riches; being held in high esteem is
better than silver or gold.
—*Proverbs 22:1 (NLT)*

Keep falsehood and lies far from me;
give me neither poverty nor riches, but
give me only my daily bread. Otherwise,
I may have too much and disown you
and say, "Who is the LORD?" Or I may
become poor and steal, and so dishonor
the name of my God.
—*Proverbs 30:8–9 (NIV)*

For You, Lord, are good, and ready to forgive, and abundant in mercy to all those who call upon You.
　　—*Psalm 86:5 (NKJV)*

Give to every person that asks you. When a person takes something that is yours, don't ask for it back.
　　—*Luke 6:30 (ERV)*

We must not become tired of doing good. We will receive our harvest of eternal life at the right time. We must not give up! When we have the opportunity to do good to any person, we should do it. But we should give special attention to the people that are in the family of believers (the church).
　　—*Galatians 6:9–10 (ERV)*

God blesses those whose hearts are pure, for they will see God.
　　—*Matthew 5:8 (NLT)*

Portrait of Goodness

Tabitha

In the city of Joppa there was a follower of Jesus named Tabitha. (Her Greek name, Dorcas, means "a deer.") She always did good things for people. She always gave money to people that needed it. While Peter was in Lydda, Tabitha became sick and died. They washed her body and put it in a room upstairs.

The followers in Joppa heard that Peter was in Lydda. (Lydda is near Joppa.) So they sent two men to Peter. They begged him, "Hurry, please come quickly!" Peter got ready and went with them. When he arrived, they took him to the room upstairs. All the widows stood around Peter. They were crying. They showed Peter the coats and other

clothes that Dorcas (Tabitha) had made
when she was still alive.

Peter sent all the people out of the
room. He kneeled and prayed. Then
he turned to Tabitha's body and said,
"Tabitha, stand up!" She opened her
eyes. When she saw Peter, she sat up.
He gave her his hand and helped her
stand up. Then he called the believers
and the widows into the room. He
showed them Tabitha; she was alive!
People everywhere in Joppa learned
about this. Many of these people
believed in the Lord (Jesus).
—*Acts 9:36–42 (ERV)*

Faithfulness

Never let loyalty and kindness leave you! Tie them around your neck as a reminder. Write them deep within your heart. Then you will find favor with both God and people, and you will earn a good reputation.

—*Proverbs 3:3–4 (NLT)*

Your kingdom is an everlasting kingdom, and your dominion endures through all generations. The LORD is faithful to all his promises and loving toward all he has made.

—*Psalm 145:13 (NIV)*

But may the God of all grace, who called us to His eternal glory by Christ Jesus, after you have suffered a while, perfect, establish, strengthen, and settle you.

—*1 Peter 5:10 (NKJV)*

He has made His wonderful works to be remembered; the LORD is gracious and full of compassion. . . . The works of His hands are verity and justice; all His precepts are sure. They stand fast forever and ever, and are done in truth and uprightness.

—*Psalm 111:4, 7–8 (NKJV)*

Never abandon a friend—either yours or your father's. When disaster strikes, you won't have to ask your brother for assistance. It's better to go to a neighbor than to a brother who lives far away.

—*Proverbs 27:10 (NLT)*

I will proclaim the name of the LORD.
Oh, praise the greatness of our God! He
is the Rock, his works are perfect, and
all his ways are just. A faithful God who
does no wrong, upright and just is he.
        —*Deuteronomy 32:3–4 (NIV)*

But the Lord is faithful. He will give you
strength and protect you from the Evil
One (the devil).
        —*2 Thessalonians 3:3 (ERV)*

If we claim to be without sin, we deceive
ourselves and the truth is not in us. If
we confess our sins, he is faithful and
just and will forgive us our sins and
purify us from all unrighteousness. If
we claim we have not sinned, we make
him out to be a liar and his word has
no place in our lives.
        —*1 John 1:8–10 (NIV)*

Your love, O LORD, reaches to the heavens, your faithfulness to the skies.
—*Psalm 36:5 (NIV)*

Understand, therefore, that the LORD your God is indeed God. He is the faithful God who keeps his covenant for a thousand generations and lavishes his unfailing love on those who love him and obey his commands.
—*Deuteronomy 7:9 (NLT)*

With the merciful You will show Yourself merciful; with a blameless man You will show Yourself blameless.
—*Psalm 18:25 (NKJV)*

Stay away from the evil things a young person wants to do. Try very hard to live right and to have faith, love, and peace. Do these things together with those people who have pure hearts and trust in the Lord.
—*2 Timothy 2:22 (ERV)*

But you, O Lord, are a compassionate and gracious God, slow to anger, abounding in love and faithfulness.
—*Psalm 86:15 (NIV)*

If you are faithful in little things, you will be faithful in large ones. But if you are dishonest in little things, you won't be honest with greater responsibilities. And if you are untrustworthy about worldly wealth, who will trust you with the true riches of heaven? And if you are not faithful with other people's things, why should you be trusted with things of your own?
—*Luke 16:10–12 (NLT)*

My eyes shall be on the faithful of the land, that they may dwell with me; He who walks in a perfect way, He shall serve me.
—*Psalm 101:6 (NKJV)*

The master was full of praise. "Well done, my good and faithful servant. You have been faithful in handling this small amount, so now I will give you many more responsibilities. Let's celebrate together!"

—*Matthew 25:21 (NLT)*

Be careful that you do not forget the LORD your God, failing to observe his commands, his laws and his decrees that I am giving you this day.

—*Deuteronomy 8:11 (NIV)*

If we are not faithful, he will still be faithful, because he cannot be false to himself.

—*2 Timothy 2:13 (ERV)*

He who calls you is faithful, who also will do it.

—*1 Thessalonians 5:24 (NKJV)*

[Be] confident of this, that he who began a good work in you will carry it on to completion until the day of Christ Jesus.

—*Philippians 1:6 (NIV)*

What's more, I am with you, and I will protect you wherever you go. One day I will bring you back to this land. I will not leave you until I have finished giving you everything I have promised you.

—*Genesis 28:15 (NLT)*

No temptation has overtaken you except such as is common to man; but God is faithful, who will not allow you to be tempted beyond what you are able, but with the temptation will also make the way of escape, that you may be able to bear it.

—*1 Corinthians 10:13 (NKJV)*

God is faithful. He is the One who has called you to share life with his Son, Jesus Christ our Lord.

—*1 Corinthians 1:9 (ERV)*

I do not hide your righteousness in my heart; I speak of your faithfulness and salvation. I do not conceal your love and your truth from the great assembly.

—*Psalm 40:10 (NIV)*

I will sing of the mercies of the LORD forever; with my mouth will I make known Your faithfulness to all generations. For I have said, "Mercy shall be built up forever; Your faithfulness You shall establish in the very heavens."

—*Psalm 89:1–2 (NKJV)*

Moreover it is required in stewards that one be found faithful.

—*1 Corinthians 4:2 (NKJV)*

Also with the lute I will praise you—
And Your faithfulness, O my God! To
You I will sing with the harp, O Holy
One of Israel.
        —*Psalm 71:22 (NKJV)*

Righteousness and justice are the
foundation of your throne. Unfailing
love and truth walk before you as
attendants.
        —*Psalm 89:14 (NLT)*

He will cover you with his feathers, and
under his wings you will find refuge;
his faithfulness will be your shield and
rampart.
        —*Psalm 91:4 (NIV)*

The Lord is good! His love is forever. We
can trust him forever and ever!
        —*Psalm 100:5 (ERV)*

I bow before your holy Temple as I worship. I praise your name for your unfailing love and faithfulness; for your promises are backed by all the honor of your name.

—*Psalm 138:2 (NLT)*

It is true that some Jews were not faithful to God. But will that stop God from doing what he promised? No! God will continue to be true even when every person is false. Like the Scriptures say: "You will be proved right in your words, and you will win when you are being judged."

—*Romans 3:3–4 (ERV)*

O LORD, You are my God. I will exalt You, I will praise Your name, for You have done wonderful things; Your counsels of old are faithfulness and truth.

—*Isaiah 25:1 (NKJV)*

Because of the LORD's great love we are not consumed, for his compassions never fail. They are new every morning; great is your faithfulness.

—*Lamentations 3:22–23 (NIV)*

But if you refuse to serve the LORD, then choose today whom you will serve. Would you prefer the gods your ancestors served beyond the Euphrates? Or will it be the gods of the Amorites in whose land you now live? But as for me and my family, we will serve the LORD.

—*Joshua 24:15 (NLT)*

You must follow the Lord your God! Respect him. Obey the Lord's commands, and do what he tells you. Serve the Lord, and never leave him!

—*Deuteronomy 13:4 (ERV)*

God is not a man, that He should lie, nor a son of man, that He should repent. Has He said, and will He not do? Or has He spoken, and will He not make it good?

—*Numbers 23:19 (NKJV)*

Only I can tell you the future before it even happens. Everything I plan will come to pass, for I do whatever I wish.

—*Isaiah 46:10 (NLT)*

Ah, Sovereign LORD, you have made the heavens and the earth by your great power and outstretched arm. Nothing is too hard for you.

—*Jeremiah 32:17 (NIV)*

Love the LORD, all you godly ones! For the LORD protects those who are loyal to him, but he harshly punishes the arrogant. So be strong and courageous, all you who put your hope in the LORD!

—*Psalm 31:23–24 (NLT)*

God's word is true. You can depend on everything he does.
—Psalm 33:4 (ERV)

But the LORD's plans stand firm forever; his intentions can never be shaken.
—Psalm 33:11 (NLT)

You who love the LORD, hate evil! He preserves the souls of His saints; He delivers them out of the hand of the wicked.
—Psalm 97:10 (NKJV)

Let us hold unswervingly to the hope we profess, for he who promised is faithful.
—Hebrews 10:23 (NIV)

He saves and protects good, honest people. He protects people who are fair to other people. He guards his holy people.
—Proverbs 2:7–8 (ERV)

The LORD leads with unfailing love and faithfulness all who keep his covenant and obey his demands.
    —*Psalm 25:10 (NLT)*

But Christ is faithful in ruling God's house like a Son. We believers are God's house (family). We are God's house if we continue to be sure and proud of the great hope we have.
    —*Hebrews 3:6 (ERV)*

Therefore let those who suffer according to the will of God commit their souls to Him in doing good, as to a faithful Creator.
    —*1 Peter 4:19 (NKJV)*

I will not violate my covenant or alter what my lips have uttered.
    —*Psalm 89:34 (NIV)*

Don't be afraid of what you are about to suffer. The devil will throw some of you into prison to test you. You will suffer for ten days. But if you remain faithful even when facing death, I will give you the crown of life.
      —*Revelation 2:10 (NLT)*

Portrait of Faithfulness
Daniel and the Lions

It pleased Darius to appoint 120
satraps to rule throughout the
kingdom, with three administrators
over them, one of whom was Daniel.
The satraps were made accountable to
them so that the king might not suffer
loss. Now Daniel so distinguished
himself among the administrators and
the satraps by his exceptional qualities
that the king planned to set him
over the whole kingdom. At this, the
administrators and the satraps tried
to find grounds for charges against
Daniel in his conduct of government
affairs, but they were unable to do
so. They could find no corruption in
him, because he was trustworthy and
neither corrupt nor negligent. Finally
these men said, "We will never find

any basis for charges against this man Daniel unless it has something to do with the law of his God."

So the administrators and the satraps went as a group to the king and said: "O King Darius, live forever! The royal administrators, prefects, satraps, advisers and governors have all agreed that the king should issue an edict and enforce the decree that anyone who prays to any god or man during the next thirty days, except to you, O king, shall be thrown into the lions' den. Now, O king, issue the decree and put it in writing so that it cannot be altered—in accordance with the laws of the Medes and Persians, which cannot be repealed." So King Darius put the decree in writing.

Now when Daniel learned that the decree had been published, he went home to his upstairs room where the windows opened toward Jerusalem. Three times a day he got down on his knees and prayed, giving thanks to his God, just as he had done before. Then these men went as a group and found Daniel praying and asking God for help. So they went to the king and spoke to him about his royal decree: "Did you not publish a decree that during the next thirty days anyone who prays to any god or man except to you, O king, would be thrown into the lions' den?"

The king answered, "The decree stands—in accordance with the laws of the Medes and Persians, which cannot be repealed."

Then they said to the king, "Daniel, who is one of the exiles from Judah, pays no attention to you, O king, or to the decree you put in writing. He still prays three times a day." When the king heard this, he was greatly distressed;

he was determined to rescue Daniel
and made every effort until sundown to
save him.

Then the men went as a group to the
king and said to him, "Remember, O
king, that according to the law of the
Medes and Persians no decree or edict
that the king issues can be changed."

So the king gave the order, and they
brought Daniel and threw him into
the lions' den. The king said to Daniel,
"May your God, whom you serve
continually, rescue you!"

A stone was brought and placed
over the mouth of the den, and the
king sealed it with his own signet ring
and with the rings of his nobles, so
that Daniel's situation might not be
changed. Then the king returned to
his palace and spent the night without
eating and without any entertainment
being brought to him. And he could not
sleep.

At the first light of dawn, the king got up and hurried to the lions' den. When he came near the den, he called to Daniel in an anguished voice, "Daniel, servant of the living God, has your God, whom you serve continually, been able to rescue you from the lions?"

Daniel answered, "O king, live forever! My God sent his angel, and he shut the mouths of the lions. They have not hurt me, because I was found innocent in his sight. Nor have I ever done any wrong before you, O king."

The king was overjoyed and gave orders to lift Daniel out of the den. And when Daniel was lifted from the den, no wound was found on him, because he had trusted in his God.

—*Daniel 6:1–23 (NIV)*

Gentleness

Let your gentleness be evident to all. The Lord is near.
>—*Philippians 4:5 (NIV)*

For the kingdom of God is not in word but in power. What do you want? Shall I come to you with a rod, or in love and a spirit of gentleness?
>—*1 Corinthians 4:20–21 (NKJV)*

Now the overseer must be above reproach, the husband of but one wife, temperate, self-controlled, respectable, hospitable, able to teach, not given to drunkenness, not violent but gentle, not quarrelsome, not a lover of money.
>—*1 Timothy 3:2–3 (NIV)*

We were not looking for praise from people. We were not looking for praise from you or any other people. We are apostles of Christ. And so when we were with you, we could have used our authority to make you do things. But we were very gentle with you. We were like a mother caring for her little children.

—*1 Thessalonians 2:6–7 (ERV)*

I, therefore, the prisoner of the Lord, beseech you to walk worthy of the calling with which you were called, with all lowliness and gentleness, with longsuffering, bearing with one another in love.

—*Ephesians 4:1–2 (NKJV)*

A servant of the Lord must not quarrel but must be kind to everyone, be able to teach, and be patient with difficult people. Gently instruct those who oppose the truth. Perhaps God will change those people's hearts, and they will learn the truth.

—*2 Timothy 2:24–25 (NLT)*

And after the earthquake there was a fire, but the LORD was not in the fire. And after the fire there was the sound of a gentle whisper.

—*1 Kings 19:12 (NLT)*

Therefore, as the elect of God, holy and beloved, put on tender mercies, kindness, humility, meekness, longsuffering.

—*Colossians 3:12 (NKJV)*

But in your hearts set apart Christ as Lord. Always be prepared to give an answer to everyone who asks you to give the reason for the hope that you have. But do this with gentleness and respect, keeping a clear conscience, so that those who speak maliciously against your good behavior in Christ may be ashamed of their slander.

—*1 Peter 3:15–16 (NIV)*

Blessed are the meek, for they will inherit the earth.

—*Matthew 5:5 (NIV)*

Take my yoke upon you. Let me teach you, because I am humble and gentle at heart, and you will find rest for your souls.

—*Matthew 11:29 (NLT)*

Patient talk can make any person change his thinking, even a ruler. Gentle talk is very powerful.
   —*Proverbs 25:15 (ERV)*

But you, O man of God, flee these things and pursue righteousness, godliness, faith, love, patience, gentleness.
   —*1 Timothy 6:11 (NKJV)*

The lowly will possess the land and will live in peace and prosperity.
   —*Psalm 37:11 (NLT)*

A peaceful answer causes anger to disappear. But a rough answer causes anger to grow.
   —*Proverbs 15:1 (ERV)*

PORTRAIT OF GENTLENESS
JESUS, THE *Gentle* KING

As Jesus and the disciples approached Jerusalem, they came to the town of Bethphage on the Mount of Olives. Jesus sent two of them on ahead. "Go into the village over there," he said. "As soon as you enter it, you will see a donkey tied there, with its colt beside it. Untie them and bring them to me. If anyone asks what you are doing, just say, 'The Lord needs them,' and he will immediately let you take them."

This took place to fulfill the prophecy that said, "Tell the people of Israel, 'Look, your King is coming to you. He is humble, riding on a donkey—riding on a donkey's colt.'"

The two disciples did as Jesus commanded. They brought the donkey and the colt to him and threw their garments over the colt, and he sat on it.

Most of the crowd spread their garments on the road ahead of him, and others cut branches from the trees and spread them on the road. Jesus was in the center of the procession, and the people all around him were shouting, "Praise God for the Son of David! Blessings on the one who comes in the name of the LORD! Praise God in highest heaven!"

The entire city of Jerusalem was in an uproar as he entered. "Who is this?" they asked.

And the crowds replied, "It's Jesus, the prophet from Nazareth in Galilee."

—*Matthew 21:1–11 (NLT)*

Self-control

For God did not give us a spirit of timidity, but a spirit of power, of love and of self-discipline.

—*2 Timothy 1:7 (NIV)*

The time is near when all things will end. So keep your minds clear, and control yourselves. This will help you to pray.

—*1 Peter 4:7 (ERV)*

For the grace of God that brings salvation has appeared to all men, teaching us that, denying ungodliness and worldly lusts, we should live soberly, righteously, and godly in the present age.

—*Titus 2:11–12 (NKJV)*

So we should not be like other people.
We should not be sleeping. We should
be awake and have self-control. People
who sleep, sleep at night. People who
get drunk, get drunk at night. But we
belong to the day (goodness), so we
should control ourselves. We should
wear faith and love to protect us. And
the hope of salvation should be our
helmet.

—*1 Thessalonians 5:6–8 (ERV)*

Therefore, prepare your minds for
action; be self-controlled; set your hope
fully on the grace to be given you when
Jesus Christ is revealed. As obedient
children, do not conform to the evil
desires you had when you lived in
ignorance. But just as he who called
you is holy, so be holy in all you do.

—*1 Peter 1:13–15 (NIV)*

Teach the older men to exercise self-control, to be worthy of respect, and to live wisely. They must have sound faith and be filled with love and patience. Similarly, teach the older women to live in a way that honors God. They must not slander others or be heavy drinkers. Instead, they should teach others what is good. These older women must train the younger women to love their husbands and their children, to live wisely and be pure, to work in their homes, to do good, and to be submissive to their husbands. Then they will not bring shame on the word of God. In the same way, encourage the young men to live wisely.

—*Titus 2:2–6 (NLT)*

A bishop then must be blameless, the husband of one wife, temperate, sober-minded, of good behavior, hospitable, able to teach.

—*1 Timothy 3:2 (NKJV)*

An elder has the job of taking care of God's work. So people should not be able to say that he lives in a wrong way. He must not be a person who is proud and selfish or who becomes angry quickly. He must not drink too much wine. He must not be a person who likes to fight. And he must not be a person who always tries to get rich by cheating people. An elder must be ready to help people by accepting them into his home. He must love what is good. He must be wise. He must live right. He must be pleasing to God. And he must be able to control himself.

—*Titus 1:7–8 (ERV)*

Stay alert! Watch out for your great enemy, the devil. He prowls around like a roaring lion, looking for someone to devour.

—*1 Peter 5:8 (NLT)*

Don't sin by letting anger control you. Think about it overnight and remain silent.

—*Psalm 4:4 (NLT)*

Like a city whose walls are broken down is a man who lacks self-control.

—*Proverbs 25:28 (NIV)*

Portrait of Self-control
The Mayor *Quiets* a Riot

About that time, serious trouble
developed in Ephesus concerning
the Way. It began with Demetrius, a
silversmith who had a large business
manufacturing silver shrines of the
Greek goddess Artemis. He kept
many craftsmen busy. He called them
together, along with others employed in
similar trades, and addressed them as
follows:

"Gentlemen, you know that our
wealth comes from this business. But
as you have seen and heard, this man
Paul has persuaded many people that
handmade gods aren't really gods at
all. And he's done this not only here
in Ephesus but throughout the entire
province! Of course, I'm not just talking

about the loss of public respect for our business. I'm also concerned that the temple of the great goddess Artemis will lose its influence and that Artemis—this magnificent goddess worshiped throughout the province of Asia and all around the world—will be robbed of her great prestige!"

At this their anger boiled, and they began shouting, "Great is Artemis of the Ephesians!" Soon the whole city was filled with confusion. Everyone rushed to the amphitheater, dragging along Gaius and Aristarchus, who were Paul's traveling companions from Macedonia. Paul wanted to go in, too, but the believers wouldn't let him. Some of the officials of the province, friends of Paul, also sent a message to him, begging him not to risk his life by entering the amphitheater.

Inside, the people were all shouting,

some one thing and some another. Everything was in confusion. In fact, most of them didn't even know why they were there. The Jews in the crowd pushed Alexander forward and told him to explain the situation. He motioned for silence and tried to speak. But when the crowd realized he was a Jew, they started shouting again and kept it up for two hours: "Great is Artemis of the Ephesians! Great is Artemis of the Ephesians!"

At last the mayor was able to quiet them down enough to speak. "Citizens of Ephesus," he said. "Everyone knows that Ephesus is the official guardian of the temple of the great Artemis, whose image fell down to us from heaven. Since this is an undeniable fact, you should stay calm and not do anything rash. You have brought these men here, but they have stolen nothing from the temple and have not spoken against our goddess.

"If Demetrius and the craftsmen have a case against them, the courts are in session and the officials can hear the case at once. Let them make formal charges. And if there are complaints about other matters, they can be settled in a legal assembly. I am afraid we are in danger of being charged with rioting by the Roman government, since there is no cause for all this commotion. And if Rome demands an explanation, we won't know what to say." Then he dismissed them, and they dispersed.

—*Acts 19:23–41 (NLT)*

THE BLESSINGS OF BEARING

the Fruit

OF THE HOLY SPIRIT

God is in the light (goodness). We should live in the light, too. If we live in the light, then we share fellowship with each other. And when we live in the light, the blood (death) of Jesus cleanses us from all sin. (Jesus is God's Son.)

—1 John 1:7 (ERV)

 WITH GOD

My soul yearns, even faints, for the courts of the LORD; my heart and my flesh cry out for the living God.
— *Psalm 84:2 (NIV)*

You also are being built together for a dwelling place of God in the Spirit.
— *Ephesians 2:22 (NKJV)*

But now in Christ Jesus you who once were far off have been brought near by the blood of Christ. . . . And He came and preached peace to you who were afar off and to those who were near. For through Him we both have access by one Spirit to the Father.
— *Ephesians 2:13, 17–18 (NKJV)*

No person has ever seen God. But if we love each other, then God lives in us. If we love each other, then God's love has reached its goal—it is made perfect in us. We know that we live in God and God lives in us. We know this because God gave us his Spirit. We have seen that the Father sent his Son to be the Savior of the world. That is what we tell people now. If a person says, "I believe that Jesus is the Son of God," then God lives in that person. And that person lives in God.

—*1 John 4:12–15 (ERV)*

I seek you with all my heart; do not let me stray from your commands. I have hidden your word in my heart that I might not sin against you.

—*Psalm 119:10–11 (NIV)*

Jesus said, "I am the true vine; my Father is the gardener. He cuts off every branch of mine that does not make fruit. And he trims and cleans every branch that makes fruit, so that it will make even more fruit. You are already clean because of the teaching I have told you. Continue in me and I will continue in you. No branch can make fruit alone. It must continue in the vine. It is the same with you. You cannot make fruit alone. You must continue in me. I am the vine and you are the branches. If a person continues in me and I continue in that person, then that person will make much fruit. But without me that person can do nothing."

—*John 15:1–5 (ERV)*

And you know that Jesus came to take away our sins, and there is no sin in him. Anyone who continues to live in him will not sin. But anyone who keeps on sinning does not know him or understand who he is.

—*1 John 3:5–6 (NLT)*

God was pleased for all of himself to live in Christ. And through Christ, God was happy to bring all things back to himself again—things on earth and things in heaven. God made peace by using Christ's blood (death) on the cross.

—*Colossians 1:19–20 (ERV)*

Because of Christ and our faith in him, we can now come boldly and confidently into God's presence.

—*Ephesians 3:12 (NLT)*

And this is His commandment: that
we should believe on the name of His
Son Jesus Christ and love one another,
as He gave us commandment. Now he
who keeps His commandments abides
in Him, and He in him. And by this we
know that He abides in us, by the Spirit
whom He has given us.

—*1 John 3:23–24 (NKJV)*

If you love me, obey my
commandments. And I will ask the
Father, and he will give you another
Advocate, who will never leave you. He
is the Holy Spirit, who leads into all
truth. The world cannot receive him,
because it isn't looking for him and
doesn't recognize him. But you know
him, because he lives with you now and
later will be in you.

—*John 14:15–17 (NLT)*

This includes you who were once far away from God. You were his enemies, separated from him by your evil thoughts and actions. Yet now he has reconciled you to himself through the death of Christ in his physical body. As a result, he has brought you into his own presence, and you are holy and blameless as you stand before him without a single fault.

—*Colossians 1:21–22 (NLT)*

If we claim to have fellowship with him yet walk in the darkness, we lie and do not live by the truth.

—*1 John 1:6 (NIV)*

Harmony WITH OTHERS

Finally, all of you, live in harmony with one another; be sympathetic, love as brothers, be compassionate and humble. Do not repay evil with evil or insult with insult, but with blessing, because to this you were called so that you may inherit a blessing.

—*1 Peter 3:8–9 (NIV)*

Be kind and loving to each other. Forgive each other the same as God forgave you in Christ.

—*Ephesians 4:32 (ERV)*

Live in harmony with each other. Don't be too proud to enjoy the company of ordinary people. And don't think you know it all!

—*Romans 12:16 (NLT)*

Open your mouth for the speechless, in the cause of all who are appointed to die. Open your mouth, judge righteously, and plead the cause of the poor and needy.

—*Proverbs 31:8–9 (NKJV)*

Then Peter came to Jesus and asked, "Lord, when my brother won't stop doing wrong to me, how many times must I forgive him? Should I forgive him as many as seven times?" Jesus answered, "I tell you, you must forgive him more than seven times. You must continue to forgive him even if he does wrong to you seventy-seven times."

—*Matthew 18:21–22 (ERV)*

Behold, how good and how pleasant it is for brethren to dwell together in unity!

—*Psalm 133:1 (NKJV)*

Young men, in the same way be submissive to those who are older. All of you, clothe yourselves with humility toward one another, because, "God opposes the proud but gives grace to the humble." Humble yourselves, therefore, under God's mighty hand, that he may lift you up in due time.

—1 Peter 5:5–6 (NIV)

So you must stop telling lies. You must always speak the truth to each other, because we all belong to each other in the same body.

—Ephesians 4:25 (ERV)

In a lawsuit, you must not deny justice to the poor. Be sure never to charge anyone falsely with evil. Never sentence an innocent or blameless person to death, for I never declare a guilty person to be innocent.

—Exodus 23:6–7 (NLT)

"These are the things you shall do: Speak each man the truth to his neighbor; give judgment in your gates for truth, justice, and peace; let none of you think evil in your heart against your neighbor; and do not love a false oath. For all these are things that I hate," says the LORD.
        —*Zechariah 8:16–17 (NKJV)*

Perfume and incense bring joy to the heart, and the pleasantness of one's friend springs from his earnest counsel.
        —*Proverbs 27:9 (NIV)*

But now you must rid yourselves of all such things as these: anger, rage, malice, slander, and filthy language from your lips. Do not lie to each other, since you have taken off your old self with its practices.
        —*Colossians 3:8–9 (NIV)*

Some people make cutting remarks,
but the words of the wise bring healing.
—*Proverbs 12:18 (NLT)*

So when you offer your gift to God,
think about other people. If you are
offering your gift before the altar, and
you remember that your brother has
something against you, then leave your
gift there at the altar. Go and make
peace with that person. Then come and
offer your gift.
—*Matthew 5:23–24 (ERV)*

Do the best you can to live in peace
with all people.
—*Romans 12:18 (ERV)*

Let each of you look out not only for his
own interests, but also for the interests
of others.
—*Philippians 2:4 (NKJV)*

An honest witness tells the truth; a false witness tells lies.
  —*Proverbs 12:17 (NLT)*

Pride only breeds quarrels, but wisdom is found in those who take advice.
  —*Proverbs 13:10 (NIV)*

Let all bitterness, wrath, anger, clamor, and evil speaking be put away from you, with all malice.
  —*Ephesians 4:31 (NKJV)*

If you have these things, then I ask you to do something for me. This will make me very happy. I ask that all your minds be joined together by believing the same things. Be joined together in your love for each other. Live together by agreeing with each other and having the same goals.
  —*Philippians 2:2 (ERV)*

Love prospers when a fault is forgiven, but dwelling on it separates close friends.

—*Proverbs 17:9 (NLT)*

The beginning of strife is like releasing water; therefore stop contention before a quarrel starts.

—*Proverbs 17:14 (NKJV)*

Therefore I exhort first of all that supplications, prayers, intercessions, and giving of thanks be made for all men, for kings and all who are in authority, that we may lead a quiet and peaceable life in all godliness and reverence.

—*1 Timothy 2:1–2 (NKJV)*

Do nothing out of selfish ambition or vain conceit, but in humility consider others better than yourselves.

—*Philippians 2:3 (NIV)*

Always be humble and gentle. Be patient and accept each other with love.
—*Ephesians 4:2 (ERV)*

Don't plot harm against your neighbor, for those who live nearby trust you. Don't pick a fight without reason, when no one has done you harm.
—*Proverbs 3:29–30 (NLT)*

We love because he first loved us. If anyone says, "I love God," yet hates his brother, he is a liar. For anyone who does not love his brother, whom he has seen, cannot love God, whom he has not seen. And he has given us this command: Whoever loves God must also love his brother.
—*1 John 4:19–21 (NIV)*

Therefore, there is now no condemnation for those who are in Christ Jesus, because through Christ Jesus the law of the Spirit of life set me free from the law of sin and death.
—*Romans 8:1–2 (NIV)*

For the LORD God is a sun and shield; the LORD will give grace and glory; no good thing will He withhold from those who walk uprightly.
—*Psalm 84:11 (NKJV)*

Yes, and the Lord will deliver me from every evil attack and will bring me safely into his heavenly Kingdom. All glory to God forever and ever! Amen.
—*2 Timothy 4:18 (NLT)*

We are hard pressed on every side,
yet not crushed; we are perplexed,
but not in despair; persecuted, but
not forsaken; struck down, but not
destroyed.

—*2 Corinthians 4:8–9 (NKJV)*

And now Jesus can help those people
who are tempted. Jesus is able to help
because he himself suffered and was
tempted.

—*Hebrews 2:18 (ERV)*

The LORD detests the way of the
wicked but he loves those who pursue
righteousness.

—*Proverbs 15:9 (NIV)*

For as the heavens are high above the
earth, so great is His mercy toward
those who fear Him.

—*Psalm 103:11 (NKJV)*

Have you never heard? Have you never understood? The LORD is the everlasting God, the Creator of all the earth. He never grows weak or weary. No one can measure the depths of his understanding. He gives power to the weak and strength to the powerless. Even youths will become weak and tired, and young men will fall in exhaustion. But those who trust in the LORD will find new strength. They will soar high on wings like eagles. They will run and not grow weary. They will walk and not faint.

—*Isaiah 40:28–31 (NLT)*

"I say this because I know the plans that I have for you." This message is from the Lord. "I have good plans for you. I don't plan to hurt you. I plan to give you hope and a good future."

—*Jeremiah 29:11 (ERV)*

The eyes of the Lord watch over those who do right, and his ears are open to their prayers. But the Lord turns his face against those who do evil.

—*1 Peter 3:12 (NLT)*

Trust the Lord completely! Don't depend on your own knowledge. Think about God in all that you do. Then he will help you.

—*Proverbs 3:5–6 (ERV)*

The LORD rescues the godly; he is their fortress in times of trouble. The LORD helps them, rescuing them from the wicked. He saves them, and they find shelter in him.

—*Psalm 37:39–40 (NLT)*

I was young and now I am old, yet I have never seen the righteous forsaken or their children begging bread.

—*Psalm 37:25 (NIV)*

The LORD is gracious and full of
compassion, slow to anger and great in
mercy. The LORD is good to all, and His
tender mercies are over all His works.
>—*Psalm 145:8–9 (NKJV)*

Good people are like the early morning
light. The sun rises and the day
becomes brighter and happier.
>—*Proverbs 4:18 (ERV)*

The name of the LORD is a strong tower;
the righteous run to it and are safe.
>—*Proverbs 18:10 (NKJV)*

O my Strength, I sing praise to you;
you, O God, are my fortress, my loving
God.
>—*Psalm 59:17 (NIV)*

I will sing of your love and justice,
LORD. I will praise you with songs.
>—*Psalm 101:1 (NLT)*

But then the kindness and love of God our Savior was made known. He saved us because of his mercy (love), not because of any good things we did. He saved us through the washing that made us new people. He saved us by making us new through the Holy Spirit. God poured out (gave) to us that Holy Spirit fully through Jesus Christ our Savior.

—*Titus 3:4–6 (ERV)*

For he will deliver the needy who cry out, the afflicted who have no one to help. He will take pity on the weak and the needy and save the needy from death.

—*Psalm 72:12–13 (NIV)*

Praise God! God did not turn away from me—he listened to my prayer. God showed his love to me!

—*Psalm 66:20 (ERV)*

The eyes of the LORD are on the righteous and his ears are attentive to their cry.
—*Psalm 34:15 (NIV)*

All of us used to live that way, following the passionate desires and inclinations of our sinful nature. By our very nature we were subject to God's anger, just like everyone else. But God is so rich in mercy, and he loved us so much, that even though we were dead because of our sins, he gave us life when he raised Christ from the dead. (It is only by God's grace that you have been saved!)
—*Ephesians 2:3–5 (NLT)*

Blessed are the undefiled in the way, who walk in the law of the LORD!
—*Psalm 119:1 (NKJV)*

Don't be impressed with your own wisdom. Instead, fear the LORD and turn away from evil. Then you will have healing for your body and strength for your bones.

—*Proverbs 3:7–8 (NLT)*

There is no God except the Lord. There is no Rock, except our God. God gives me strength. He helps me live a pure life.

—*Psalm 18:31–32 (ERV)*

Finally, I confessed all my sins to you and stopped trying to hide my guilt. I said to myself, "I will confess my rebellion to the LORD." And you forgave me! All my guilt is gone.

—*Psalm 32:5 (NLT)*

He who conceals his sins does not prosper, but whoever confesses and renounces them finds mercy.

—*Proverbs 28:13 (NIV)*

The Lord is my Rock, my Fortress, my Place of Safety. My God is my Rock. I run to him for protection. God is my shield. His power saves me. The Lord is my hiding place high in the hills.

—Psalm 18:2 (ERV)

Commit your way to the LORD; trust in him and he will do this: He will make your righteousness shine like the dawn, the justice of your cause like the noonday sun.

—Psalm 37:5–6 (NIV)

The way of the Lord is a stronghold to those with integrity, but it destroys the wicked.

—Proverbs 10:29 (NLT)

Say to the righteous that it shall be well with them, for they shall eat the fruit of their doings.

—Isaiah 3:10 (NKJV)

The righteousness of the blameless makes a straight way for them, but the wicked are brought down by their own wickedness.

—*Proverbs 11:5 (NIV)*

The way of the godly leads to life; that path does not lead to death.

—*Proverbs 12:28 (NLT)*

What great blessings there are for the people that want to do right more than anything else! God will fully satisfy them.

—*Matthew 5:6 (ERV)*

But I will sing of your strength, in the morning I will sing of your love; for you are my fortress, my refuge in times of trouble.

—*Psalm 59:16 (NIV)*

The work of righteousness will be peace, and the effect of righteousness, quietness and assurance forever.

—*Isaiah 32:17 (NKJV)*

Give to other people, and you will receive. You will be given much. It will be poured into your hands—more than you can hold. You will be given so much that it will spill into your lap. The way you give to other people is the way God will give to you.

—*Luke 6:38 (ERV)*

A little that a righteous man has is better than the riches of many wicked. For the arms of the wicked shall be broken, but the LORD upholds the righteous.

—*Psalm 37:16–17 (NKJV)*

The godly can look forward to a reward, while the wicked can expect only judgment.
> —*Proverbs 11:23 (NLT)*

God says there is one thing you can really depend on (and I believe it): "Strength comes from God!" My Master, your love is real. You reward or punish a person for the things he does.
> —*Psalm 62:11–12 (ERV)*

For he who sows to his flesh will of the flesh reap corruption, but he who sows to the Spirit will of the Spirit reap everlasting life.
> —*Galatians 6:8 (NKJV)*

He replied, "Blessed rather are those who hear the word of God and obey it."
> —*Luke 11:28 (NIV)*

Lord, when you do good things to good people, you are like a large shield protecting them.

—*Psalm 5:12 (ERV)*

You did not choose Me, but I chose you and appointed you that you should go and bear fruit, and that your fruit should remain, that whatever you ask the Father in My name He may give you.

—*John 15:16 (NKJV)*

The LORD gives his people strength. The LORD blesses them with peace.

—*Psalm 29:11 (NLT)*

An *Effective,* FRUITFUL LIFE

Try to live in peace with all people. And try to live lives free from sin. If a person's life is not holy, then he will never see the Lord.

—Hebrews 12:14 (ERV)

After they prayed, the place where they were meeting was shaken. And they were all filled with the Holy Spirit and spoke the word of God boldly.

—Acts 4:31 (NIV)

Pray in the Spirit at all times and on every occasion. Stay alert and be persistent in your prayers for all believers everywhere.

—Ephesians 6:18 (NLT)

Suppose you see a brother or sister who has no food or clothing, and you say, "Good-bye and have a good day; stay warm and eat well"—but then you don't give that person any food or clothing. What good does that do?

—*James 2:15–16 (NLT)*

He who trusts in his riches will fall, but the righteous will flourish like foliage.

—*Proverbs 11:28 (NKJV)*

The things a good man does are like the Tree of Life. A wise man gives new life to people.

—*Proverbs 11:30 (ERV)*

Let love be without hypocrisy. Abhor what is evil. Cling to what is good. Be kindly affectionate to one another with brotherly love, in honor giving preference to one another.

—*Romans 12:9–10 (NKJV)*

So then, just as you received Christ Jesus as Lord, continue to live in him, rooted and built up in him, strengthened in the faith as you were taught, and overflowing with thankfulness.

—*Colossians 2:6–7 (NIV)*

God blesses those who work for peace, for they will be called the children of God.

—*Matthew 5:9 (NLT)*

Therefore, as the elect of God, holy and beloved, put on tender mercies, kindness, humility, meekness, longsuffering; bearing with one another, and forgiving one another, if anyone has a complaint against another; even as Christ forgave you, so you also must do. But above all these things put on love, which is the bond of perfection.

—*Colossians 3:12–14 (NKJV)*

Dear friends, since God so loved us, we also ought to love one another.
—*1 John 4:11 (NIV)*

Though I am free and belong to no man, I make myself a slave to everyone, to win as many as possible. To the Jews I became like a Jew, to win the Jews. To those under the law I became like one under the law (though I myself am not under the law), so as to win those under the law. To those not having the law I became like one not having the law (though I am not free from God's law but am under Christ's law), so as to win those not having the law. To the weak I became weak, to win the weak. I have become all things to all men so that by all possible means I might save some.
—*1 Corinthians 9:19–22 (NIV)*

And you yourself must be an example to them by doing good works of every kind. Let everything you do reflect the integrity and seriousness of your teaching. Teach the truth so that your teaching can't be criticized. Then those who oppose us will be ashamed and have nothing bad to say about us.

—*Titus 2:7–8 (NLT)*

Let this mind be in you which was also in Christ Jesus, who, being in the form of God, did not consider it robbery to be equal with God, but made Himself of no reputation, taking the form of a bondservant, and coming in the likeness of men. And being found in appearance as a man, He humbled Himself and became obedient to the point of death, even the death of the cross.

—*Philippians 2:5–8 (NKJV)*

The righteous considers the cause of the poor, but the wicked does not understand such knowledge.
—*Proverbs 29:7 (NKJV)*

Now, people of Israel, listen! What does the Lord your God really want from you? The Lord wants you to respect him and do what he says. God wants you to love him and to serve the Lord your God with all your heart and with all your soul. So obey the laws and commands of the Lord that I am giving you today. These laws and commands are for your own good.
—*Deuteronomy 10:12–13 (ERV)*

But be sure to fear the LORD and serve him faithfully with all your heart; consider what great things he has done for you.
—*1 Samuel 12:24 (NIV)*

God called us to be holy. He does not want us to live in sin.
—*1 Thessalonians 4:7 (ERV)*

If anyone speaks, let him speak as the oracles of God. If anyone ministers, let him do it as with the ability which God supplies, that in all things God may be glorified through Jesus Christ, to whom belong the glory and the dominion forever and ever. Amen.
—*1 Peter 4:11 (NKJV)*

Don't change yourselves to be like the people of this world. But let God change you inside with a new way of thinking. Then you will be able to decide and accept what God wants for you. You will be able to know what things are good and pleasing to God and what things are perfect.
—*Romans 12:2 (ERV)*

Only a person who lives a pure life,
and does good things, and speaks
truth from the heart can live on your
mountain. That kind of person doesn't
say bad things about other people.
That person doesn't do bad things to
his neighbors. That person doesn't
tell shameful things about his own
family. That person doesn't respect the
people that hate God. But that person
shows honor to all the people who
serve the Lord. If he makes a promise
to his neighbor, then he does what he
promised to do. If that person gives
money to someone, he will not charge
interest on that loan. And that person
will not take money to do bad things to
innocent people. If a person lives like
that good man, then he will always be
near God.
　　　—Psalm 15:2–5 (ERV)

But the noble man makes noble plans, and by noble deeds he stands.
　　　—*Isaiah 32:8 (NIV)*

"In your anger do not sin": Do not let the sun go down while you are still angry, and do not give the devil a foothold.
　　　—*Ephesians 4:26–27 (NIV)*

And do not present your members as instruments of unrighteousness to sin, but present yourselves to God as being alive from the dead, and your members as instruments of righteousness to God.
　　　—*Romans 6:13 (NKJV)*

For God is not unjust. He will not forget how hard you have worked for him and how you have shown your love to him by caring for other believers, as you still do.
　　　—*Hebrews 6:10 (NLT)*

Brothers and sisters, continue to think about the things that are good and worthy of praise. Think about the things that are true and honorable and right and pure and beautiful and respected.

—*Philippians 4:8 (ERV)*

Thus says the LORD: "Stand in the ways and see, and ask for the old paths, where the good way is, and walk in it; then you will find rest for your souls. But they said, 'We will not walk in it.'"

—*Jeremiah 6:16 (NKJV)*

Be kindly affectionate to one another with brotherly love, in honor giving preference to one another; not lagging in diligence, fervent in spirit, serving the Lord.

—*Romans 12:10–11 (NKJV)*